The Rarest Penguin and the *Enchanted* Galápagos Islands

A Book by Grandma Science

Copyright © 2014 Sharon F. Johnson Ph.D.
All rights reserved.

ISBN: 1497483425
ISBN 13: 9781497483422
Library of Congress Control Number: 2014906297
CreateSpace Independent Publishing Platform
North Charleston, South Carolina

Dedication

To My Grandchildren –
Bennett, Will, and especially Kate…
She thinks little penguins are totally great!

Introducing Galápagos

For all nature lovers, this book is for you.
We're off to a place that's a natural zoo.

Six hundred miles from Ecuador's shore –
the Isles of Galápagos we'll search and explore.

To sail the Pacific we'll hop on our boat –
from island to island we'll happily float.

To Seymour, Española, and Isabela –
we'll need lots of water and our travel umbrella.

We'll look for rare penguins few people have seen.
We'll pack our binocs and a lot of sunscreen.

How lucky we are this new and bright day
to search for rare creatures in a land far away.

Galápagos is commonly pronounced: Gă-lă-pă-gus.
Yes, that last syllable rhymes with the word "bus"!

Note: The image on the next page was taken by a NASA satellite in 2002.
Grandma Science modified the image to include the names and labels.

Use NASA's map to help you trace
a sailing route to each island's place.

Galapagos Islands
(Ecuador)

The Rarest Penguin
and the
Enchanted Galápagos Islands

It's off to Galápagos to explore and search
    for one of the rarest penguins on Earth!
The isle named *Seymour* – our first destination.
    What will we find at this distant location?

We'll hike its marked trails and stay along side
    our expert Galápagos Park Ranger and Guide.
We'll look all around – down low, then up high,
    And hope that a little rare penguin we'll spy.

But it's not a rare penguin that catches our eye.
It's a bird with blue feet who's not very shy.

It's a Blue-footed Booby! That's right! That's its name!
It has garnered its full share of crazy bird fame.
It's named for the color of its webbed, clown-like feet
that strut up and down to its mating dance beat.

Go ahead. It's okay. Laugh right out loud.
    This bird doesn't mind…it's got much to be proud.
It's awkward on land but not when it flies.
    It's renown for the way that it glides and plunge dives.

Well, almost as silly as it sits in a tree
    is the look of the smaller **Red-footed Booby.**

While **Blue-foots** fish in the sea by the shore,
    Red-foots prefer the deep ocean's roar.
They hunt for their fish far out at sea
    to bring back to a chick - in a nest - in a tree.

Now, another new bird has caught our attention.
Its ballooning red chest is beyond comprehension!

It's a **Great Frigatebird** that roosts in a tree
  after feeding and flying for days out at sea.
The male's puffy red chest will attract a fine mate.
  She'll lay just one egg that they'll both *incubate.*

Here's an incredible, unbelievable fact!
And it has to do with how **Frigatebirds** act!

The **Frigates** are pirates – they'd rather just steal
    a fish from another seabird's next meal.
As they circle and soar, they're on the hunt
    for a **Blue-foot** who swallowed a fish for its lunch!

With a whish and a swoop, **Frigates** don't hesitate
    to force a **Blue Booby** to regurgitate!
While still on the wing, **Frigates** snatch up the fish.
    The **Blue-foot** escapes. But it's lost its fish dish.

Although the Isles are on the Equator,
you won't see a croc or a green alligator.

But if you're not careful, you'll step right on top
    of **well-camouflaged** lizards shaped like a mop!
These **cold-blooded reptiles** keep themselves warm
    by huddling together – on the rocks – in a swarm.

They're unique among lizards. They're **Iguanas – Marine**!
That means they like water that's salty – saline.

Some call them ugly. Some say, "Oh! Gross!"
    But they're harmless, fine creatures. They'll let you get close.
In the world of iguanas, they're the rarest of rare.
    They'll pose nicely for pictures. They don't mind or care.

They move slowly on land as they seek the sea's water.
　　　Then gracefully swim – a lot like an otter.
A flat nose and sharp teeth allow them to feed
　　　on red and green algae – their favorite seaweed.

It's been a good day of hiking and scouting.
   Tomorrow we're off on another park outing.
Time to swim and relax and take a long snooze.
   There are many more islands to see on our cruise.

What's to be found at our new destination?
Will penguins abound at our second location?

It's *Española!* A most special site.
    It's the home of a rare bird that's brown, gray and white.
Endemic to this flat Galápagos Isle,
    the **Waved Albatross** has its own unique style.

Look! Look! Over there! Up in the sky!
A **Waved Albatross** is flying so high!
Breathtakingly elegant – it glides through the air.
We're amazed at the sight of a bird that's so rare.

It's the largest
   of birds
     that breeds
       only here.
On this desolate isle
   it has little
     to fear.

Standing three feet high
   it displays
     its webbed feet,
a flattened white head,
   and hooked,
     yellow beak.

We're amazed to spy on the rockiest ground
  an **Albatross** chick just looking around.
For hours and days it is left all alone
  as its parents seek food to bring back to its home.

When ready to fly, the chick walks to a ledge –
then opens its wings and soars off the edge.

It stays out at sea or heads for the shore
    of coastal Peru or warm Ecuador.
After four to six years, it returns on a quest
    to raise its own chick in lava rock nest.

What's that we hear? It sounds like a "GAWK!"
Well, look what we've found – A **Galápagos Hawk**.

With its hooked, yellow beak and sharp, *taloned* feet,
   it tears at the meat of the food that it eats.
As *scavenger – predator*, it fights to survive.
   It eats almost everything – dead or alive.

We're off to the beach of a stunning blue bay.
Could this be a good place for penguins to play?

Oh, my! What an awesome, unexpected surprise!
Galápagos Sea Lions – resting their eyes.

Sea lions have long, whiskery snouts,
And knobby, small earflaps that wiggle about.

On land, they move slowly by hopping along.
    But in the blue ocean, they're sturdy and strong.
These swift moving **mammals** are sea-going zippers.
    They swim like a bird using wing-like front flippers.

Next stop – *Isabela* –
   with
     its seahorse-like
     shape.

It's known for its
   scenic,
   geologic landscape.

There's active
   volcanoes
   and
   large **lava flows**.
And, brackish lagoons
   where
   mangrove trees
   grow.

It's off on the trail
   to a volcanic
   peak.

Could this be the home
   of the
   penguins
   we seek?

Look, Look! Over There! What's that red spot?
A **Vermilion Flycatcher's** landed on top
of a **Giant Land Tortoise** that's made a rest stop.

These **Giants** differ by the shape of their shells.
And by the island that each **Tortoise** dwells.

Some tortoise *species* have a well-rounded dome.
　　It suits those who live in a wet and moist home.
They can't reach up high for a leaf in a tree.
　　But they can eat the grass on the land by the sea.

The **Galápago –** or saddle-backed kind,
is always an amazing, fantastical find.

Their shell shape allows them to stretch their necks high
    for leaves in the trees when the islands are dry.
In fact, these rare creatures gained fame and acclaim
    by lending their name to the whole island chain.

Now back down the trail to the coast and the ocean.
Tides ebb and flow with the sea's constant motion.

Over time wind and water create lava ridges –
    crevices, caves, ledges, and bridges!
Such a wonder that barren rocks by the sea
    are a place where so many creatures live free.

Oh, My! There's a creature with legs on her side.
She seems to be waiting, but not for a ride.

It's **Sally, the Lightfooted**, scarlet-red **Crab**.
    She's hunting for lunch on a water-soaked slab.
She's easy to spot - so light on her feet.
    But as we approach, she's quick to retreat.

As we scramble on rocks and explore each ravine,
we stumble upon a fairytale scene.

A little lagoon – so calm and serene -
　　resembling a crystal of aquamarine.
It's nestled among volcanic black rock
　　with a bright, blue rowboat afloat at its dock.

Now, what will we spy if we take the blue boat?
Will we find penguin life in a place so remote?

As we float the lagoon we catch a good view
of long-legged birds with a soft, pinkish hue.

They're **Greater Flamingos**, the tallest of birds.
    They live in a place where their call's rarely heard.
Their soft pinkish color reflects what they eat –
    shrimpy *crustaceans* - their favorite treat.

As we pass by the shore we all point and stare
    at a bird that's drying its wings in the air.
It's a **Great Blue Heron** that's so statuesque
    with its feathered display and brownish-white vest.

The **Heron's** large wings are in starkest contrast
 to the **Flightless**, less-stylish, brown **Cormorant**.
Its ragged, small wings won't allow it to soar.
 But its strong feet and legs help it swim by the shore.

Now what's that I hear making such a loud squawk?
Quick, Quick! Over there! By that craggy, black rock!

It's the little rare **Penguin** we've searched and searched for.
There's one! And, there's two! *Could there be a few more?*

They're ***well-camouflaged*** in their feathered tuxedos.
    They dive, swim and glide like streamlined torpedoes.
They lay eggs in a cave of black lava rock
    where they raise just one chick to add to the flock.

Yes, the **Galápagos Penguin** lives and grows
in a place where it never freezes or snows.

It lives with the **Boobies, red-footed and blue** –
    with **sea lions, crabs** and **Waved Albatross** too.
It lives with the **hawks** with the sharpest of toes –
    with **herons, iguanas** and **pink flamingos**.
It lives with the **Frigates** by the sea's rocky shore –
    with the rarest of **cormorants** and so many more.

Now, it's back to the boat to snooze and to dream
of all the unusual creatures we've seen.
Tomorrow we'll go to the islands next door.
What more will we find as we seek and explore?

Perhaps a new Booby with brownish gray feet
and a black-ringed mask 'round its yellowish beak.

Or maybe a bird with a long, feathered tail
that uses its wings to soar and to sail.

Or an orange, spotted lizard that's just made a run
up a scaly iguana with its nose to the sun.

For it's not just rare penguins that bring on a smile
    and keep tourists hiking for many a mile.
It's ALL of the ***species*** – so rare, so unique –
    that surprise and amaze the travelers we meet…
And add to the islands' enchanted mystique.

The Tale of Volcanic Galápagos

Volcanic islands arise from the deep ocean floor
    as molten, hot rock pushes up from Earth's core.
Now this takes time – millions of years –
    before the first sign of an island appears.

Large natural rafts of plants and debris
    break off from the continent – float out to sea.
These rafts carry plants, reptiles, and more.
    And some make their way to an island's bare shore.

Eventually birds find their way to the land
    bringing seeds that grow plants in the volcanic sand.
Each island becomes its own unique place.
    Creatures fight to survive in their own special space.

Later men set to sea to explore and survey
    each island, sea coast, and sailable bay.
About 1505, the first men came ashore
    to note the location and open the door
for other seafarers to settle or moor.

Volcano: *A vent that breaks through the Earth's surface and spews liquid rock or lava. As the liquid rock cools, it produces volcanic or igneous rocks.*

Geology: *The study of Earth's history, features and materials. Some types of geologists study how islands form.*

Darwin and Galápagos

In 1835, a British sea exploration
    made Galápagos a most noted location.
A ship called **The Beagle** carried on board
    a young man named **Darwin** who kept a record.

Darwin noted the strange and unusual creatures
    that survived on each island with different features.
Back at his home, he wrote a few books
    of the lands' and the animals' unique and rare looks.

Yes, Darwin was first to observe and describe
    some of the rarest creatures alive.
Perhaps he's best known for his study of **Finch** –
    Small birds he named for their beak and their *niche*.

He noticed a finch with a beak long and curved
    made a home in a cactus where flowers were served.
A larger black finch with an oversized beak
    searched through the soil for the seeds that it eats.

The **Finches** were named – **The Cactus** and **Ground.**
    They're two **Darwin Finches** sure to be found.
That's why there's a stamp with two birds and a face
    to commemorate Darwin's Galápagos place.

To sustain and promote wildlife conservation there's **The Charles Darwin Research Station**. On *Santa Cruz Isle* it's the perfect location to continue your Galápagos wildlife education.

Want to Learn More?

*If you're still very curious, just take some time.
Here's some reasonable facts that don't have a rhyme.*

Species: A group of animals that all are alike. They mate or breed only with each other. Each animal in this book is its own species. For example, the Red-footed Booby and Blue-footed Booby are different bird species. They do not breed with each other. The Masked or Nazca Booby (page 35) is a third species of Booby.

Endemic Species: Animals that are found in one place. For example, the Galápagos Penguin is found only in the Galápagos and nowhere else. Other endemic Galápagos species are: Marine Iguana, Galápagos Hawk, Flightless Cormorant, Galápagos Giant Tortoise, Sally Lightfoot Crab, Lava Lizard (page 37), and Waved Albatross.

Endangered Species are animals (and plants) that are in danger of becoming extinct – meaning gone forever. Animals are endangered for different reasons. For example, the Galápagos Penguins number about 2000. They have the smallest population of any penguin species. Thus, slight changes in their environment endanger the whole species. Penguins need cold ocean currents to bring them enough food to survive and breed. When ocean currents warm for long periods of time (El Niño Event), food becomes scarce. The penguins breed less. If penguin numbers get too low, not enough baby penguins are born and survive to breed. Thus, the penguins are in danger of becoming extinct.

Species Extinction: Man and the introduction of domestic animals has endangered all Galápagos Giant Tortoise species. Some tortoise species are already extinct. In the 1800's, whalers killed hundreds of tortoises. The tortoises were used for food and lamp oil. In the 1900's, Galápagos settlers brought goats and other animals. The goats ate and destroyed the food and habitat of the tortoises.

Lonesome George: The last survivor of the Pinta Island tortoise species was brought to the Charles Darwin Research Center on Santa Cruz Island. He was named Lonesome George! His species became extinct on June 24, 2012, when George died of natural causes. He was believed to be more than 100 years old.

Unordinary Vocabulary

There may be more words that you don't know the meaning.
That's fine. It's okay. You should learn from your reading.
Just pretend that you are a detective or scout
who searches, defines, and figures words out.

Camouflage (cam•ou•flage): The ability to blend in with the environment. Well-camouflaged animals are less likely to be killed by predators. Penguins and iguanas are definitely well-camouflaged in Galápagos.
Did you find 6 penguins on page 32?

Crustacean (crus•ta•cean): Part of a group of animals without backbones that have a hard, outside, shell-like skeleton, jointed legs, and bodies in parts or segments. The Sally Lightfoot Crab and shrimp are crustaceans.

Incubate (in•cu•bate): Bird eggs need to be kept warm until they hatch. The female and/or male keep the eggs warm by sitting on them until the egg hatches. In other words, they 'incubate' the egg.

Mammal (mam•mal): Animal group with backbones that breathe air, have fur or hair, provide milk for their young, and are warm-blooded. A mammal's body temperature stays the same all the time and is regulated from within. (Sea lions and us!)

Niche (niche): A specie's place in the animal/plant community where it lives. It includes all the resources in its habitat – both living (other animals/plants) and non-living (type of soil/amount of rainfall).

Predator (pred•a•tor): An animal that catches, kills and eats other animals for food. Many animals in this book are predators. Most catch, kill and eat fish.

Reptile (rep•tile): Animal group with backbones that breathe air, have scales, and lay eggs on land. Their body temperature is warmed or cooled by the environment. Iguanas and snakes are cold-blooded reptiles. They warm their bodies on the rocks in the sun.

Scavenger (scav•eng•er): An animal that eats dead animals for food. The Galápagos Hawk eats dead animals that it didn't kill.

Talon (tal•on): The sharp, tearing claw of a bird.

Resources and References

Charles Darwin Foundation for the Galápagos Islands (CDF). 1959. Accessed March 18, 2014. http://www.charlesdarwinfoundation.org

This well-respected group works to protect, preserve, and sustain the environment and the wide-variety of rare *species* found in the Galápagos. The CDF conducts scientific research to help us make educated decisions about wildlife issues. The CDF built **The Charles Darwin Research Station**, a popular tourist spot on Santa Cruz Island. It has many educational programs. A visit to the tortoise feeding and breeding area is a special experience.

Galápagos National Park (GNP). 1959. Accessed March 18, 2014. http://www.Galápagospark.org

The Ecuadorian government works to conserve and sustain both population growth and tourism. The GNP manages the National Park and the Marine Reserve. The many GNP Programs target areas of greatest need. For example, some GNP programs control new *species* coming into the island. The GNP carefully monitors tourism by requiring all visitors to the islands to be accompanied by a GNP trained guide. Much of the information in this book was related to me by my excellent Ecuadorian guide.

Two Good Books:
Both books are filled with detailed information and written for adults, but their pictures and drawings are exceptional and of interest to all ages.

Fitter, J., Fitter, D., and D. Hosking. 2000. *The Wildlife of the Galápagos*. Princeton, NJ: University Press.

Heinzel, H. and B. Hall. 2000. *Galápagos Diary: A Complete Guide to the Archipelago's Birdlife*. Berkeley, CA: University of California Press.

Who is Grandma Science?

Grandma Science is me – Sharon F. Johnson, Ph.D.
    I'm a retired science educator and grandmother of three.
I hike and I bike and I travel and roam.
    Then write at my desk when I'm back in my home.
My writings are meant for all generations
    who want to explore amazing locations.
Here I am at the Darwin Research Station.
    Observing rare tortoises – my new avocation!

About Grandma Science's Books

My books are for kids – both the young and the old –
to read and to learn as they're happily told.

Please read them aloud. Sound out every word.
Each book's meant to be poetically heard.

Read them fast. Read them slow. Read them in parts.
Read them straight through or make stops and restarts.

Look closely at pictures. Describe what you see.
Ask questions and wonder, "Now how can that be?"

Look up new words – so utterly odd.
Use dictionaries or digital pods.

For more information and additional knowledge
visit a library, aquarium, museum, or college.

It's hoped that my books will open the door
to wondrous new places to seek and explore.

If you liked this book, you might also like Grandma Science's *The Littlest Beach and The Great Coral Reef*. It takes the reader on a beach walk and reef snorkel where amazing animals are discovered. It also promotes reef conservation and protection.